THIS IS MINE.
I OWN THIS!

AT ANY GIVEN MOMENT

YOU HAVE THE

POWER

TO SAY

"This is not how my story is going to end"

Guide To Your Journal

The journey from the past to a new life is just that...a journey. This journey will be fraught with twists and turns as well as high peaks and amazing views.

The aim of this journal is to be a practical and beneficial tool for you to use as you navigate through to a new life. It's a guide for you to use to live life more consciously...figure out your triggers and your drivers then decide what you want more of and less of in your life.

So much of what drives us is based on our emotions, feelings, and our thoughts around them which can be determined by a limitless number of factors. The goal is to discover what propels you so you can take control of where you're going!

Weather
Often something as simple as the weather can affect your mood. So start there...what's the weather like?

Daily activities
Keep track of what is happening in your life and how you are honestly emotionally responding to those events...good and bad. Sometimes the feeling might seem foreign, almost alien, but note it down. It can be pure gold! Knowing how you feel at different times of the day will help you identify triggers.

Triggers
What events make you happy, content, upset, feel isolated or even tempted to quit trying to make a new life for yourself? Take the time to deeply explore your reactions. After you've looked back on your day and your changing emotions throughout the day in conjunction with the associated events, write down what triggered the good and bad feelings?

Finding Joy
Life is never all good or all bad which means there is always something to be grateful for every day. What happened that created joy and put a smile on your face?

Cathartic Creativity
Turn the page over, express yourself and release what you're holding inside. The dot grid allows you to express your creativity with either words or drawing. This is your opportunity to let the inside out...whatever that may be. Let go of any pent up feelings that you might be finding difficult to process. Let this be a safe place to release your emotions!

Here's to a new start!

DATE:

TODAY'S EVENTS BIG & SMALL

*

*

*

*

FEELING ALIEN

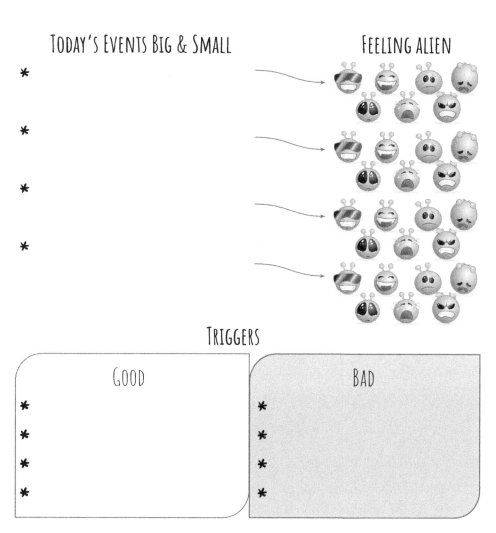

TRIGGERS

GOOD

*
*
*
*

BAD

*
*
*
*

FINDING JOY

Date:

Today's Events Big & Small   ## Feeling alien

*

*

*

*

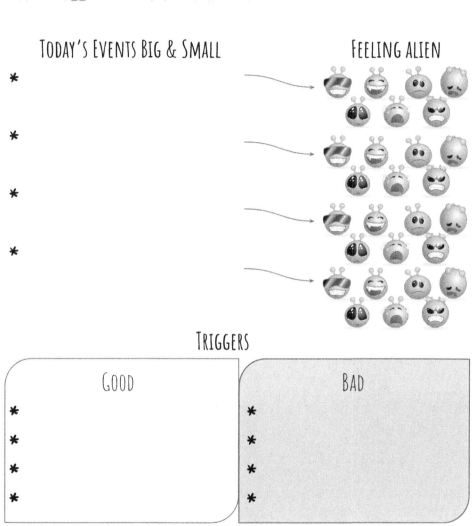

Triggers

Good
*
*
*
*

Bad
*
*
*
*

Finding Joy

DATE:

TODAY'S EVENTS BIG & SMALL

*

*

*

*

FEELING ALIEN

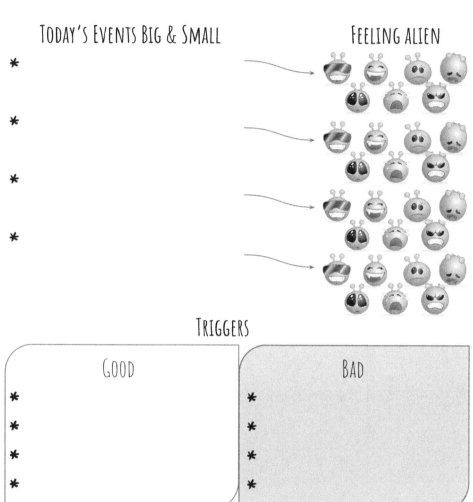

TRIGGERS

GOOD	BAD
*	*
*	*
*	*
*	*

FINDING JOY

Date:

Today's Events Big & Small

*

*

*

*

Feeling alien

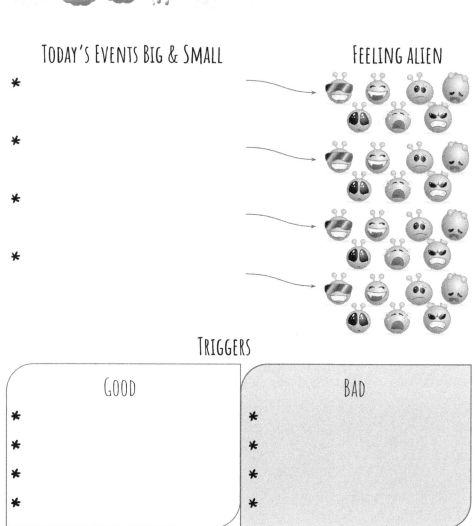

Triggers

Good
*
*
*
*

Bad
*
*
*
*

Finding Joy

DATE:

TODAY'S EVENTS BIG & SMALL

*

*

*

*

FEELING ALIEN

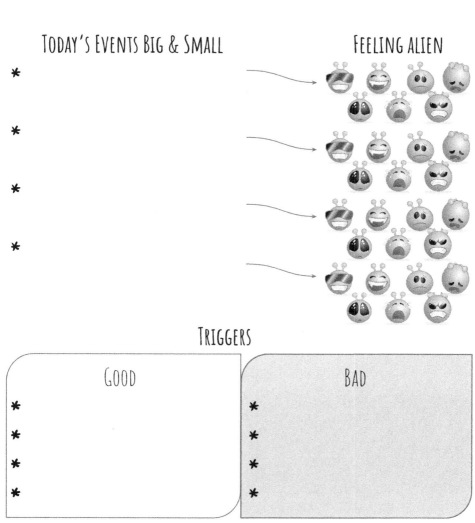

TRIGGERS

GOOD	BAD
*	*
*	*
*	*
*	*

FINDING JOY

DATE:

Today's Events Big & Small

*

*

*

*

Feeling alien

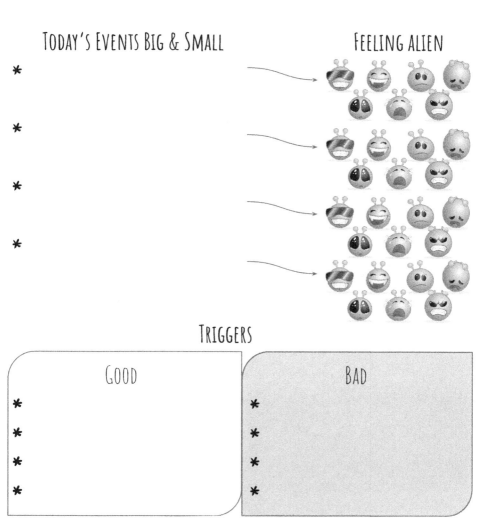

Triggers

Good

*
*
*
*

Bad

*
*
*
*

Finding Joy

Date:

Today's Events Big & Small

*

*

*

*

Feeling alien

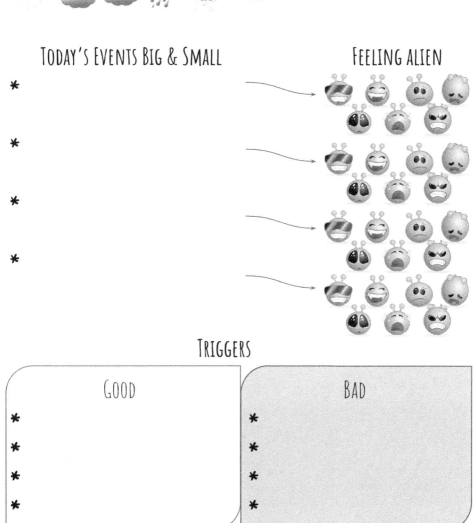

Triggers

Good	Bad
*	*
*	*
*	*
*	*

Finding Joy

Date:

Today's Events Big & Small

*

*

*

*

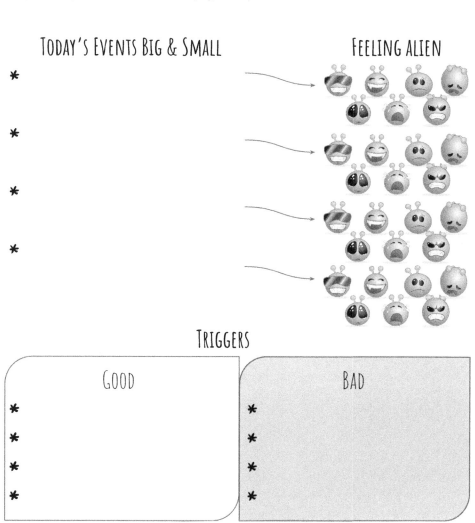

Feeling alien

Triggers

Good	Bad
*	*
*	*
*	*
*	*

Finding Joy

DATE:

Today's Events Big & Small

*

*

*

*

Feeling alien

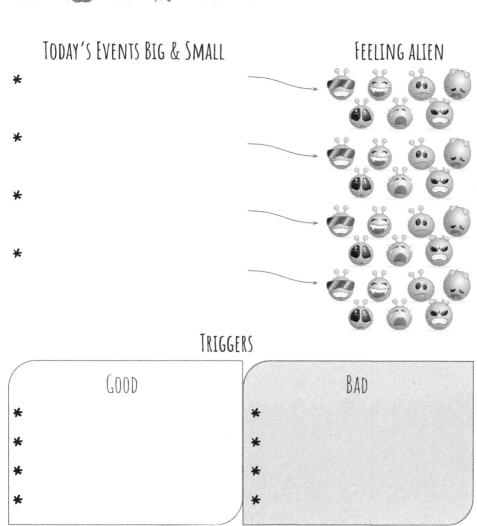

Triggers

Good

*
*
*
*

Bad

*
*
*
*

Finding Joy

DATE:

Today's Events Big & Small

*

*

*

*

Feeling alien

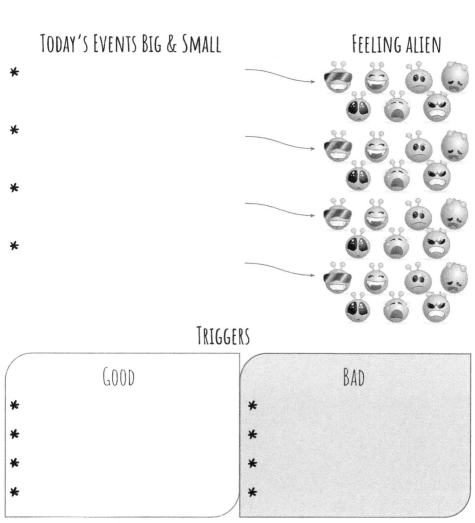

Triggers

Good

*
*
*
*

Bad

*
*
*
*

Finding Joy

DATE:

TODAY'S EVENTS BIG & SMALL

*

*

*

*

FEELING ALIEN

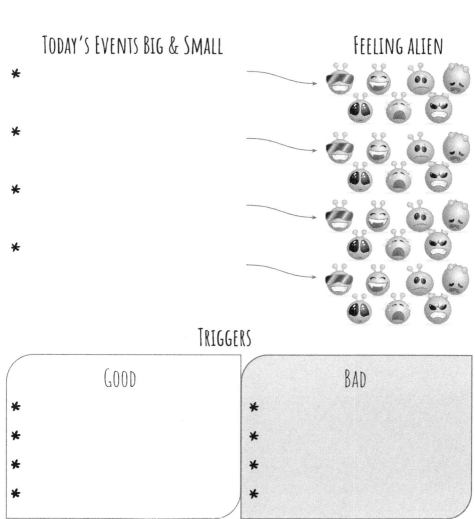

TRIGGERS

GOOD	BAD
*	*
*	*
*	*
*	*

FINDING JOY

DATE:

Today's Events Big & Small

*

*

*

*

Feeling alien

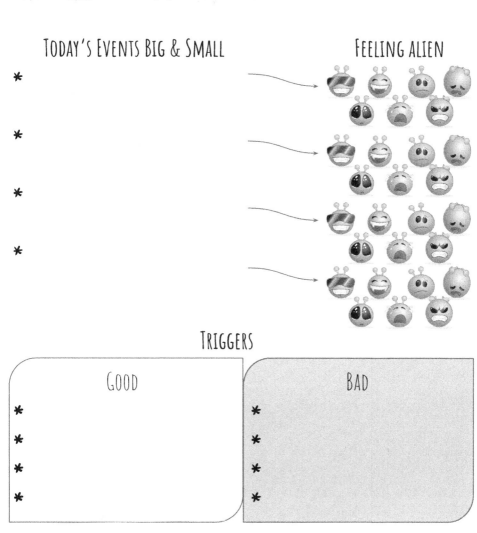

Triggers

Good	Bad
*	*
*	*
*	*
*	*

Finding Joy

Date:

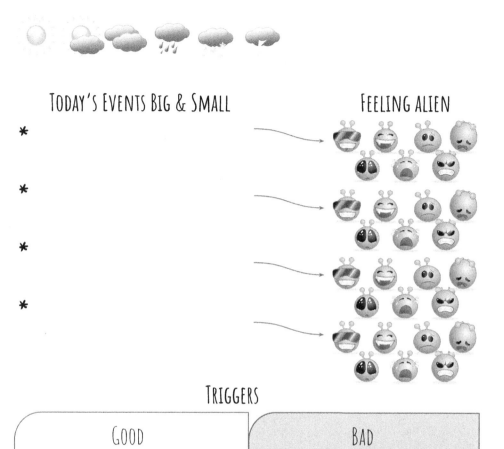

Today's Events Big & Small

*

*

*

*

Feeling alien

Triggers

Good	Bad
*	*
*	*
*	*
*	*

Finding Joy

DATE:

Today's Events Big & Small

*

*

*

*

Feeling alien

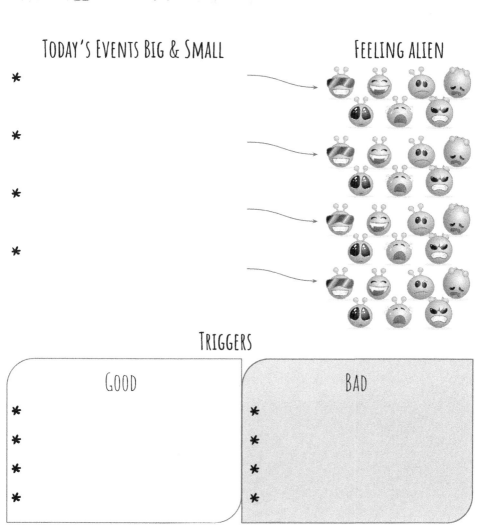

Triggers

Good	Bad
*	*
*	*
*	*
*	*

Finding Joy

Date:

Today's Events Big & Small

*

*

*

*

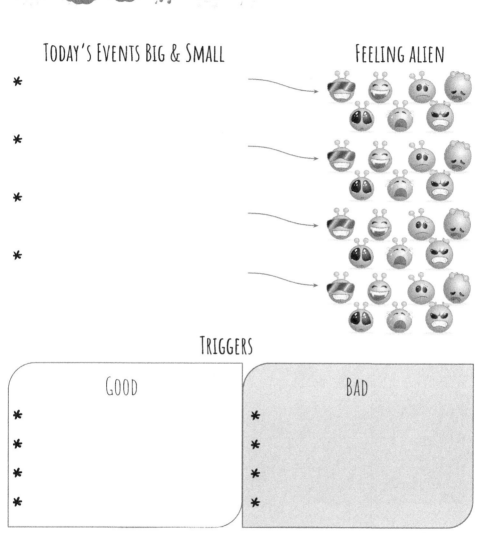

Feeling alien

Triggers

Good	Bad
*	*
*	*
*	*
*	*

Finding Joy

DATE:

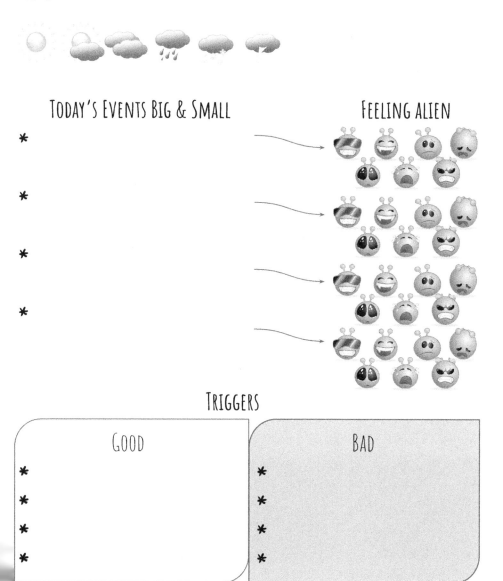

Today's Events Big & Small

*

*

*

*

Feeling alien

Triggers

Good

*
*
*
*

Bad

*
*
*
*

Finding Joy

Date:

Today's Events Big & Small

*

*

*

*

Feeling alien

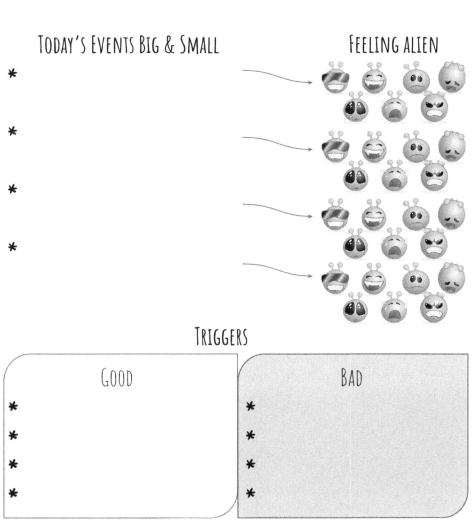

Triggers

Good	Bad
*	*
*	*
*	*
*	*

Finding Joy

DATE:

Today's Events Big & Small

*

*

*

*

Feeling alien

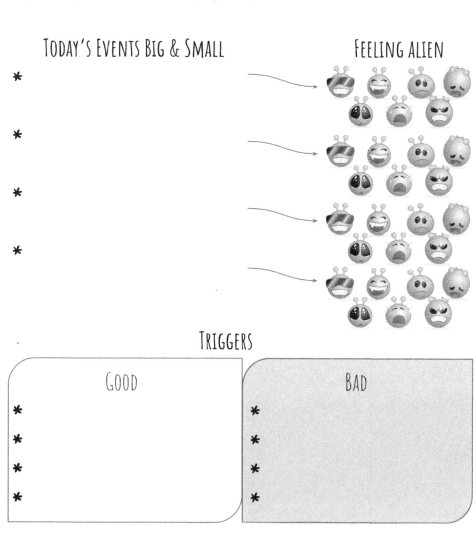

Triggers

Good	Bad
*	*
*	*
*	*
*	*

Finding Joy

Date:

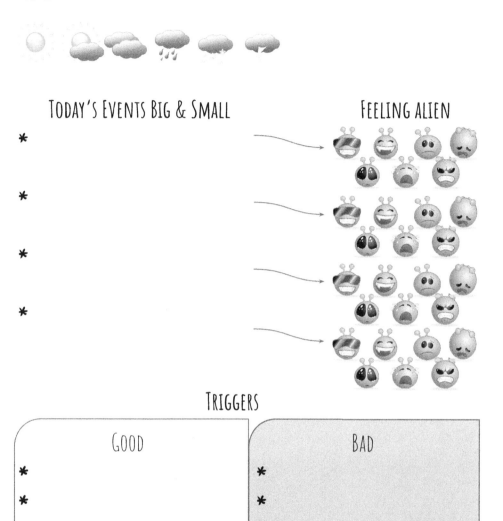

Today's Events Big & Small

*

*

*

*

Feeling alien

Triggers

Good

*

*

*

*

Bad

*

*

*

*

Finding Joy

DATE:

TODAY'S EVENTS BIG & SMALL

*

*

*

*

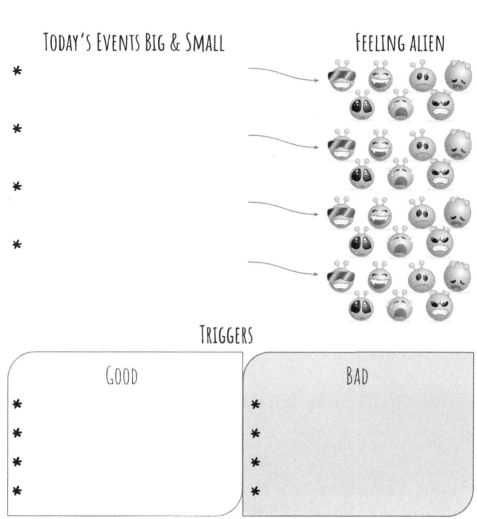

FEELING ALIEN

TRIGGERS

GOOD	BAD
*	*
*	*
*	*
*	*

FINDING JOY

DATE:

TODAY'S EVENTS BIG & SMALL

*

*

*

*

FEELING ALIEN

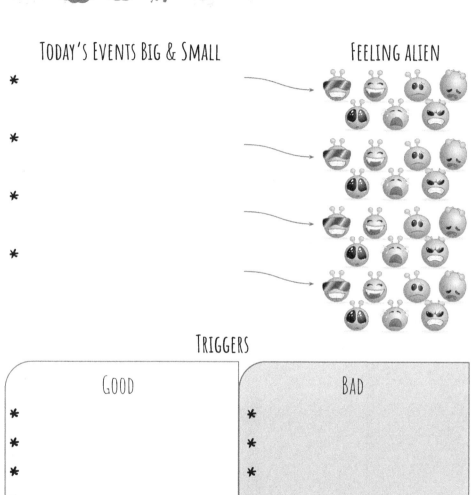

TRIGGERS

GOOD
*
*
*
*

BAD
*
*
*
*

FINDING JOY

DATE:

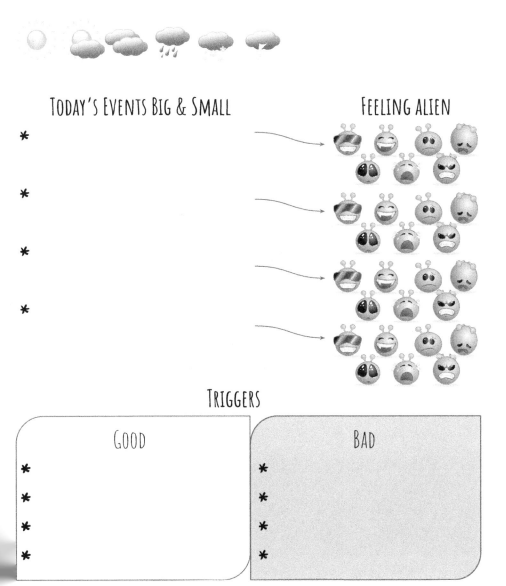

Today's Events Big & Small

*

*

*

*

Feeling alien

Triggers

Good
*
*
*
*

Bad
*
*
*
*

Finding Joy

DATE:

Today's Events Big & Small

*

*

*

*

Feeling alien

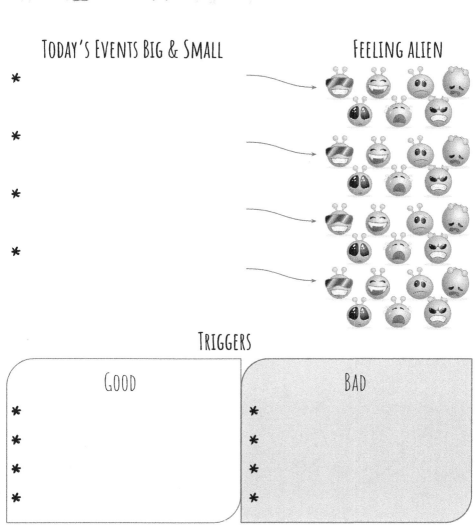

Triggers

Good

*

*

*

*

Bad

*

*

*

*

Finding Joy

DATE:

Today's Events Big & Small

*

*

*

*

Feeling alien

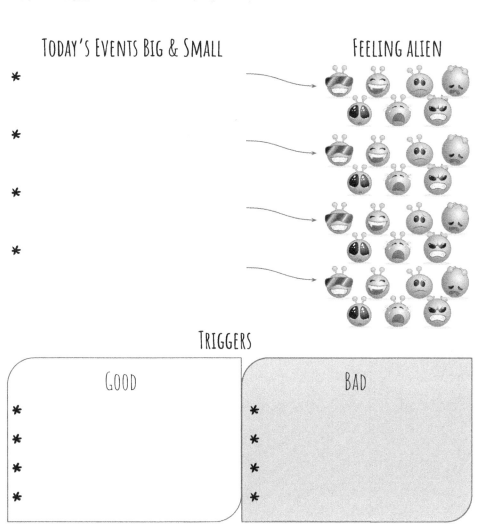

Triggers

Good

*
*
*
*

Bad

*
*
*
*

Finding Joy

Date:

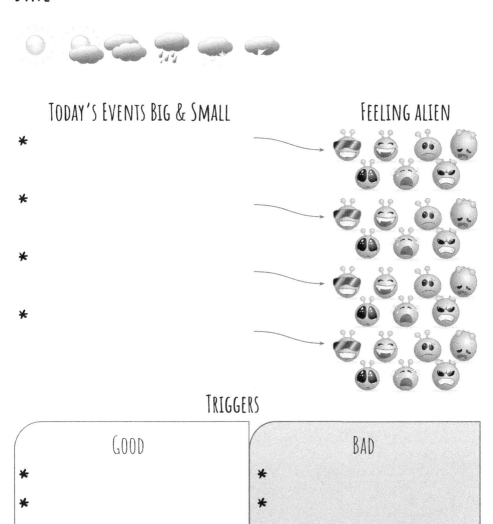

Today's Events Big & Small

*

*

*

*

Feeling alien

Triggers

Good	Bad
*	*
*	*
*	*
*	*

Finding Joy

DATE:

Today's Events Big & Small

*

*

*

*

Feeling alien

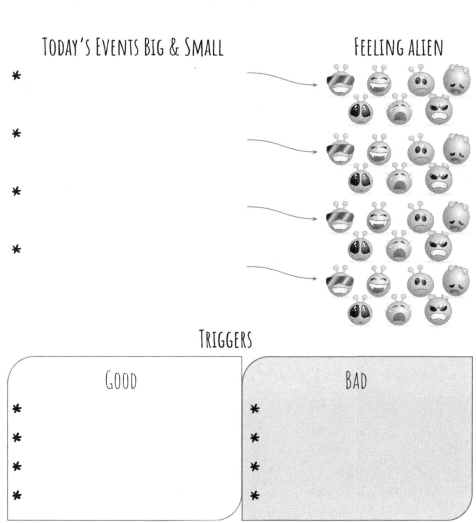

Triggers

Good	Bad
*	*
*	*
*	*
*	*

Finding Joy

DATE:

Today's Events Big & Small

*

*

*

*

Feeling alien

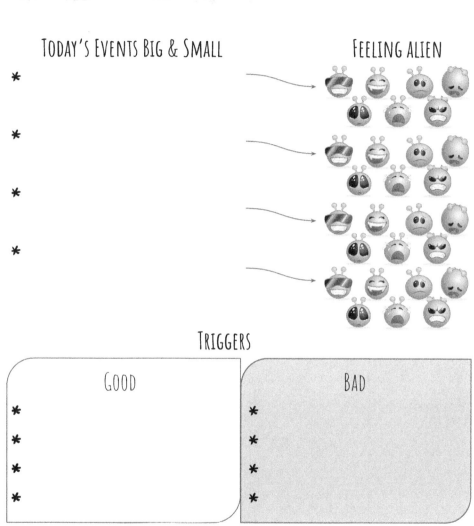

Triggers

Good	Bad
*	*
*	*
*	*
*	*

Finding Joy

DATE:

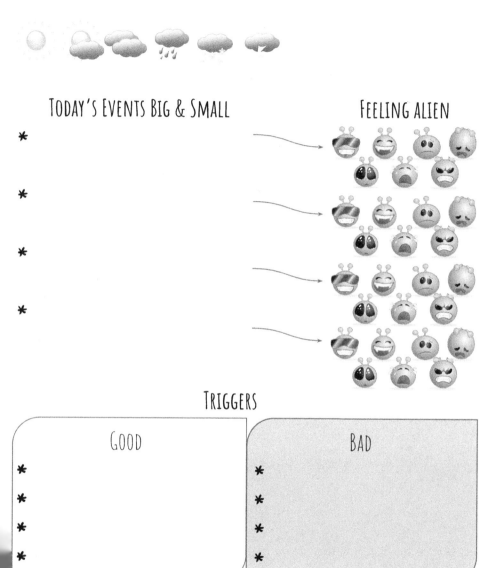

TODAY'S EVENTS BIG & SMALL

*

*

*

*

FEELING ALIEN

TRIGGERS

GOOD

*
*
*
*

BAD

*
*
*
*

FINDING JOY

DATE:

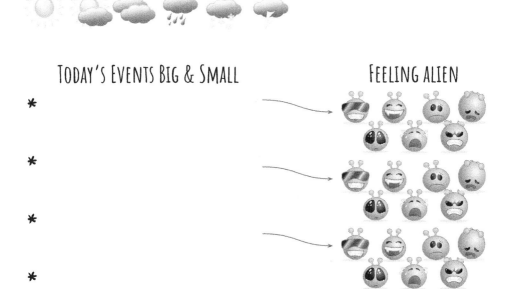

Today's Events Big & Small

*

*

*

*

Feeling alien

Triggers

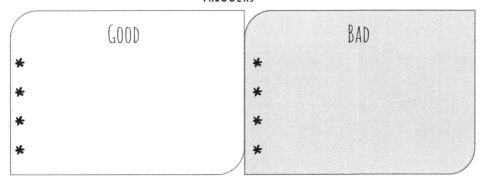

	Good		Bad
*			*
*			*
*			*
*			*

Finding Joy

DATE:

Today's Events Big & Small

*

*

*

*

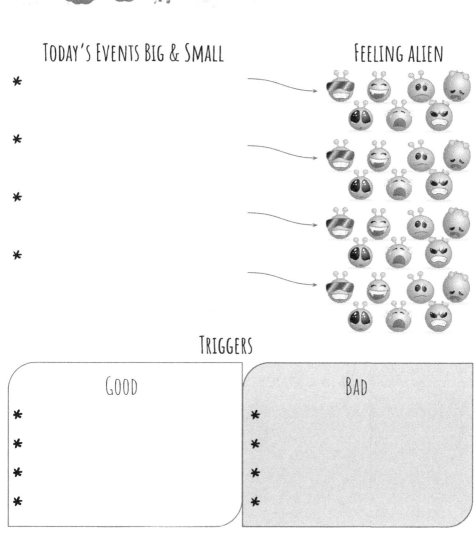

Feeling alien

Triggers

Good	Bad
*	*
*	*
*	*
*	*

Finding Joy

_____

_____

_____

Date:

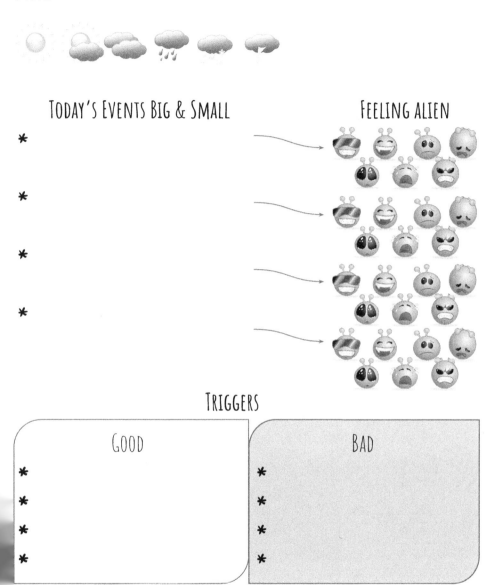

Today's Events Big & Small

*

*

*

*

Feeling alien

Triggers

Good	Bad
*	*
*	*
*	*
*	*

Finding Joy

Date:

Today's Events Big & Small

*

*

*

*

Feeling alien

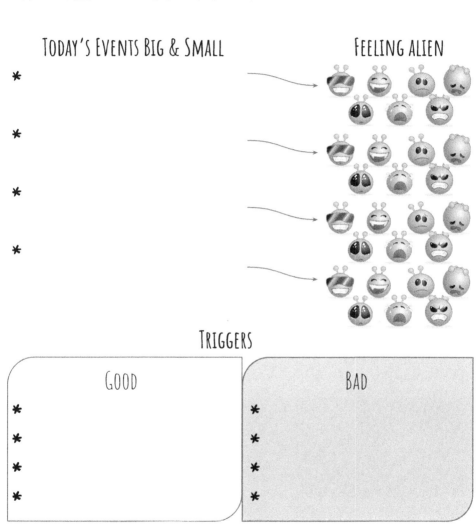

Triggers

Good	Bad
*	*
*	*
*	*
*	*

Finding Joy

DATE:

Today's Events Big & Small

*

*

*

*

Feeling alien

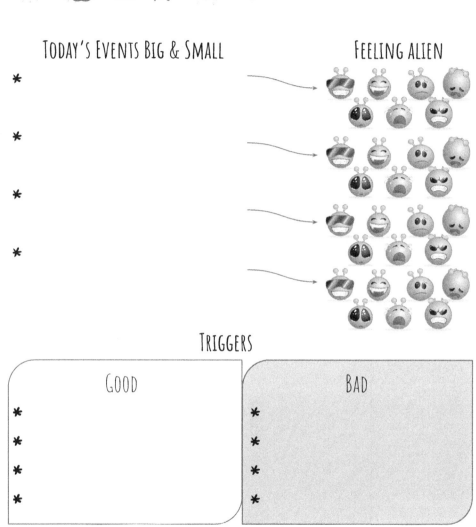

Triggers

Good

*
*
*
*

Bad

*
*
*
*

Finding Joy

DATE:

Today's Events Big & Small

*

*

*

*

Feeling alien

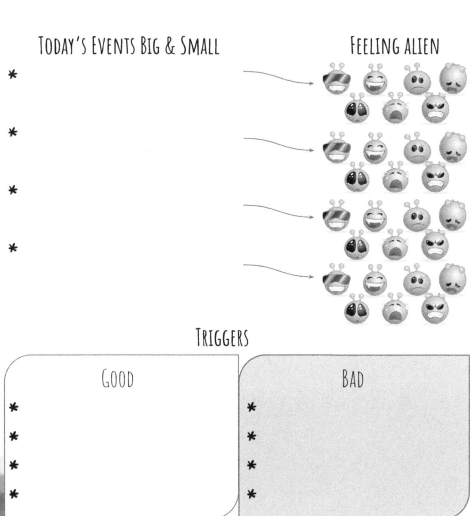

Triggers

Good	Bad
*	*
*	*
*	*
*	*

Finding Joy

DATE:

TODAY'S EVENTS BIG & SMALL

*

*

*

*

FEELING ALIEN

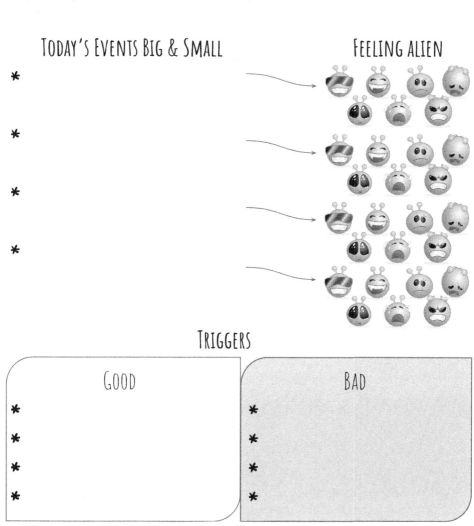

TRIGGERS

GOOD	BAD
*	*
*	*
*	*
*	*

FINDING JOY

DATE:

Today's Events Big & Small

*

*

*

*

Feeling alien

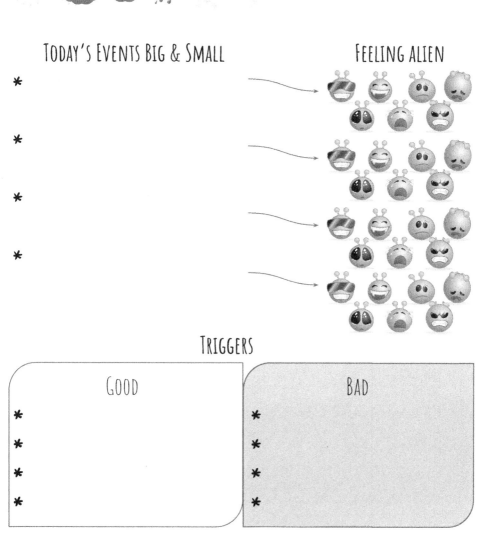

Triggers

Good

*
*
*
*

Bad

*
*
*
*

Finding Joy

DATE:

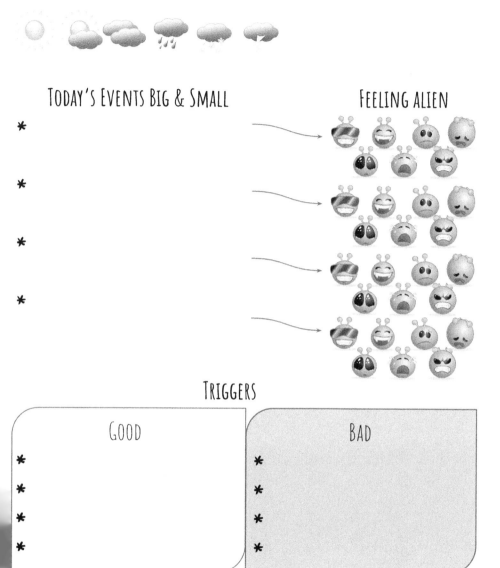

TODAY'S EVENTS BIG & SMALL

*

*

*

*

FEELING ALIEN

TRIGGERS

GOOD

*
*
*
*

BAD

*
*
*
*

FINDING JOY

Date:

Today's Events Big & Small

*

*

*

*

Feeling alien

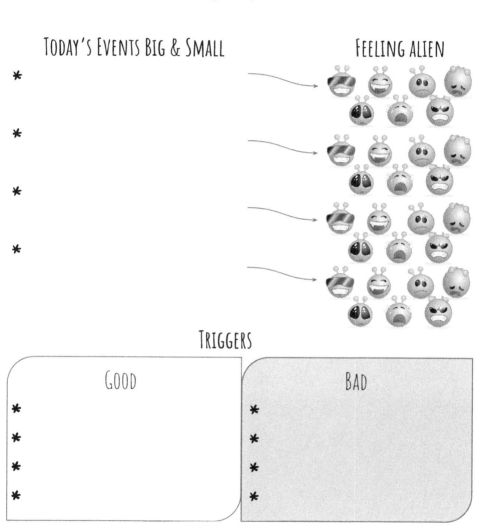

Triggers

Good	Bad
*	*
*	*
*	*
*	*

Finding Joy

DATE:

Today's Events Big & Small

*

*

*

*

Feeling alien

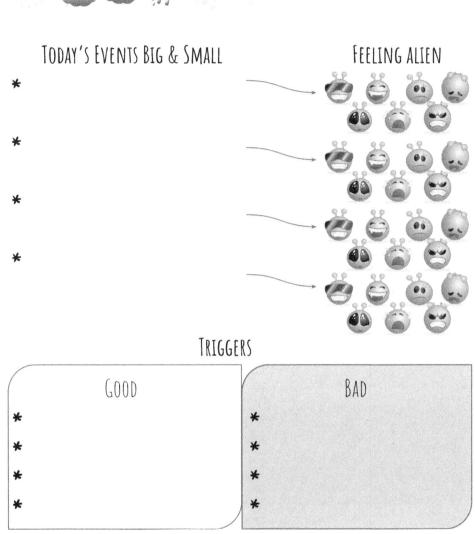

Triggers

Good	Bad
*	*
*	*
*	*
*	*

Finding Joy

_____

_____

_____

DATE:

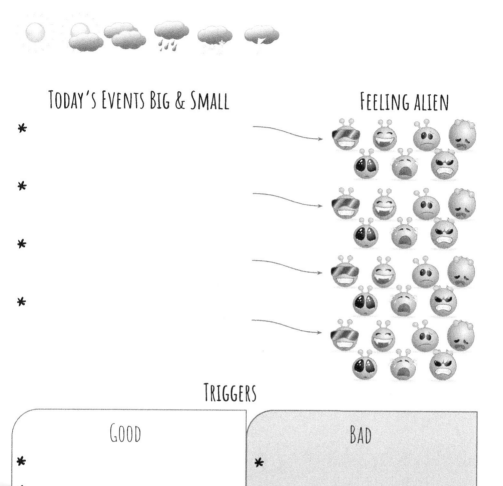

TODAY'S EVENTS BIG & SMALL

*

*

*

*

FEELING ALIEN

TRIGGERS

GOOD
*
*
*
*

BAD
*
*
*
*

FINDING JOY

DATE:

TODAY'S EVENTS BIG & SMALL

*

*

*

*

FEELING ALIEN

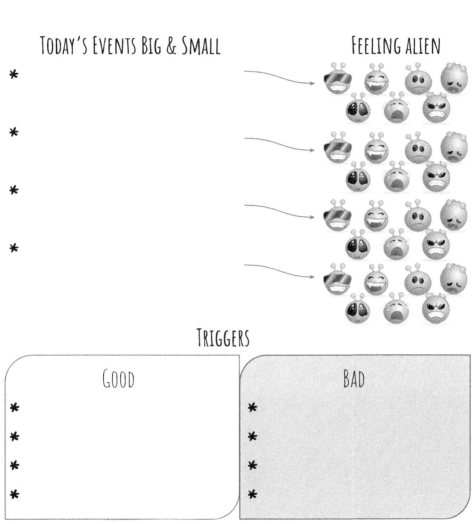

TRIGGERS

GOOD
*
*
*
*

BAD
*
*
*
*

FINDING JOY

DATE:

Today's Events Big & Small

*

*

*

*

Feeling alien

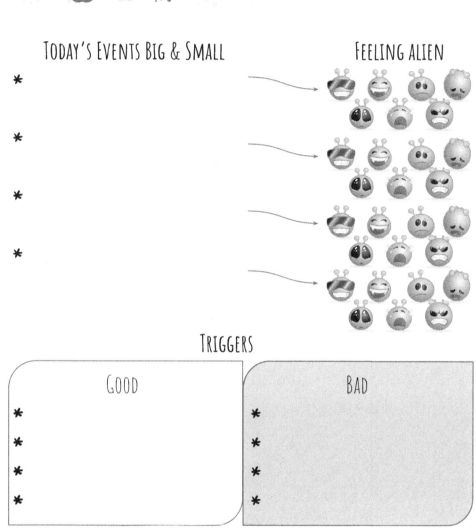

Triggers

Good	Bad
*	*
*	*
*	*
*	*

Finding Joy

DATE:

Today's Events Big & Small

*

*

*

*

Feeling alien

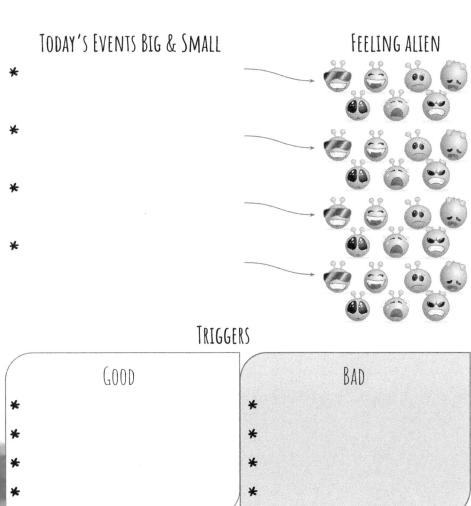

Triggers

Good	Bad
*	*
*	*
*	*
*	*

Finding Joy

DATE:

TODAY'S EVENTS BIG & SMALL

*

*

*

*

FEELING ALIEN

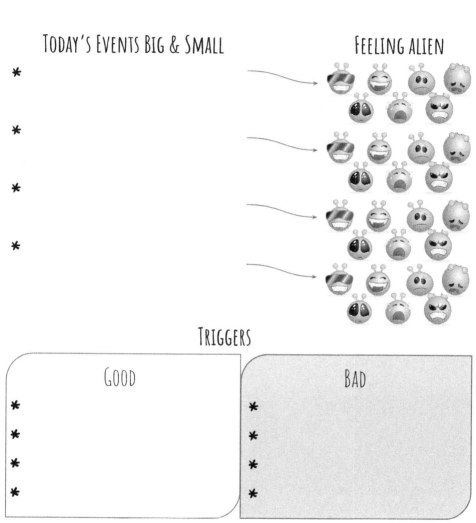

TRIGGERS

GOOD	BAD
*	*
*	*
*	*
*	*

FINDING JOY

Date:

Today's Events Big & Small

*

*

*

*

Feeling alien

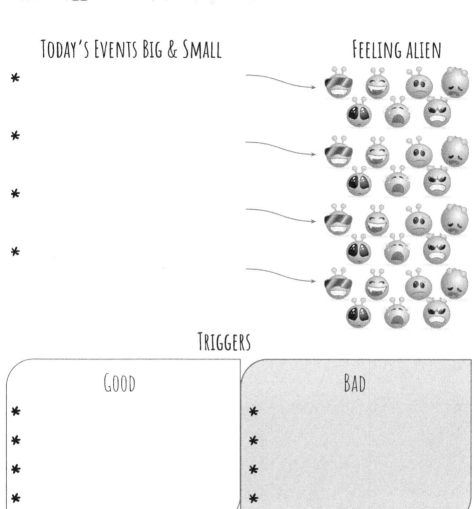

Triggers

Good	Bad
*	*
*	*
*	*
*	*

Finding Joy

DATE:

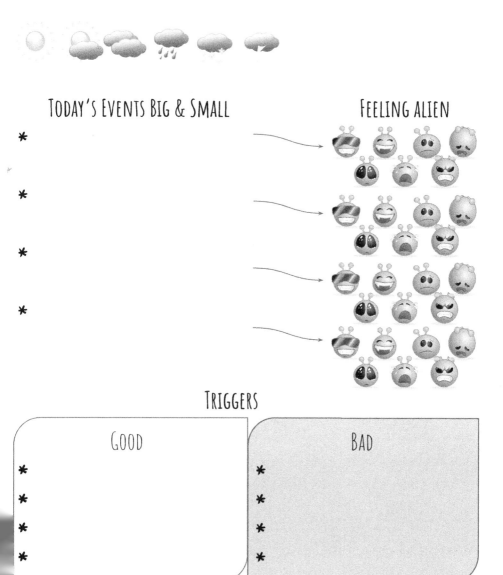

Today's Events Big & Small

*

*

*

*

Feeling alien

Triggers

Good	Bad
*	*
*	*
*	*
*	*

Finding Joy

DATE:

TODAY'S EVENTS BIG & SMALL

*

*

*

*

FEELING ALIEN

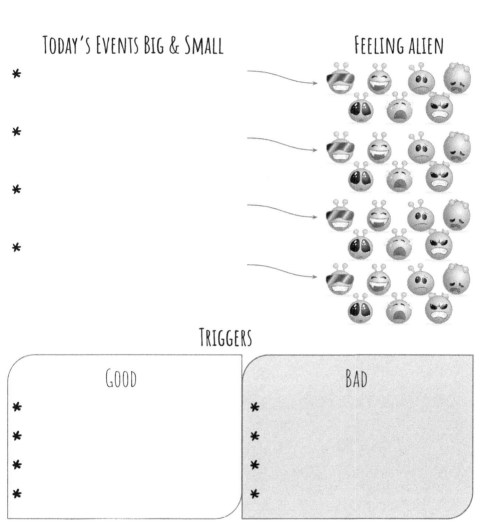

TRIGGERS

GOOD	BAD
*	*
*	*
*	*
*	*

FINDING JOY

Made in the USA
Las Vegas, NV
10 December 2024

13583619R00056